I0843988

The Custom Protocol Creator

Mastering Protocol-Oriented Programming

Table of Contents

1. Introduction 1

2. Protocol-Oriented Programming: An Introduction 2

    2.1. Understanding the Basics 2

    2.2. The Origin of Protocol-Oriented Programming 2

    2.3. What Makes POP Unique? 3

    2.4. Key Components of Protocol-Oriented Programming 3

3. Protocols 4

4. Protocol Adoption 5

5. Protocol Extensions 6

6. Protocol Inheritance 7

    6.1. Practical Applicability of Protocol-Oriented Programming . . . 7

7. The Evolution of Object-Oriented to Protocol-Oriented 9

    7.1. Encapsulation and Data Hiding 9

    7.2. Inheritance 9

    7.3. Polymorphism 10

    7.4. Introduction to Protocol-Oriented Programming 10

    7.5. Protocols and Structs 10

    7.6. Protocol Extensions 11

    7.7. Protocol Composition 11

    7.8. The Paradigm Shift 11

8. Understanding Protocols: The Backbone of POP 13

    8.1. What are Protocols? 13

    8.2. Conforming to Protocols 14

    8.3. Protocol Inheritance 14

    8.4. Protocol Composition 15

    8.5. Extending Protocols 15

    8.6. Protocols as Type 16

    8.7. Using Protocol Conformance in Practice 16

9. Creating Custom Protocols: First Steps 18

  9.1. Understanding Protocols 18

  9.2. Protocol Properties 19

  9.3. Protocol Methods 19

  9.4. Protocol Adoption 20

  9.5. Protocols as Types 20

  9.6. Inheritance in Protocols 21

10. Implementing Multiple Protocol Inheritance 22

  10.1. Understanding Multiple Protocol Inheritance 22

  10.2. Working with Multiple Protocol Inheritance 23

  10.3. Practical Use Case of Multiple Protocol Inheritance . . . 24

  10.4. Key Considerations for Implementing Multiple Protocol
Inheritance 26

11. POP in Practice: Real-World Use Cases 27

  11.1. Understanding Swift Protocols 27

  11.2. Protocols In Networking 27

  11.3. Leveraging POP in UI 28

  11.4. Protocols for Multi-Threading 28

12. Mastering Protocol Extensions 31

  12.1. Getting Started with Protocol Extensions 31

  12.2. The Benefit of Using Protocol Extensions 32

  12.3. When to Use Protocol Extensions 32

  12.4. How to Override Default Behavior 33

  12.5. Making the Most of Protocol Extensions 33

13. Optimizing Software Design with Protocols 35

  13.1. Protocol Oriented Design 35

  13.2. Extension Driven Development 36

  13.3. Adopting Protocol Compositions 37

    13.3.1. Multiprotocol Approach 37

    13.3.2. Protocol Composition Type 38

13.4. Protocol and Associated Types 38

14. Effective Strategies for Debugging Protocols 40

14.1. Understanding Protocol Behaviors 40

14.2. Debugging with Protocol Extensions 41

14.3. Inspecting Protocol Compliance 42

14.4. Debugging Inherited Protocols 42

14.5. Debugging Optional Protocol Methods 43

15. Futuristic Perspectives: The Impact of POP on Emerging
Languages 45

15.1. How POP Influences Language Constructs 45

15.2. Case Study: Swift 45

15.3. Future Prospects Influenced by POP 46

15.4. Adaptability to the Internet of Things (IoT) 46

15.5. Synergy with Microservices Architecture 47

15.6. Conclusion 47

Chapter 1. Introduction

Special Report: The Custom Protocol Creator - Mastering Protocol-Oriented Programming

Delving into the world of abstract structuring and fine-tuning systems, our specially curated report on 'The Custom Protocol Creator: Mastering Protocol-Oriented Programming' provides an in-depth overlook for both budding and established programmers who are keen on mastering this trailblazing computing paradigm. While the subject at its core is inherently technical, we promise an accessible guide not shrouded in complexity but illuminated with simplicity. This report seamlessly intertwines the fundamentals of protocol-oriented programming with its practical applicability, ensuring the reader has a concrete grasp of custom protocol creation. Acquiring this special report is the smart step towards becoming adept at crafting resilient and efficient software architectures. So, traverse into this absorbing realm of protocols, interfaces and extensions, where each page unfolds into a step closer to proficiency in protocol-oriented programming.

Chapter 2. Protocol-Oriented Programming: An Introduction

Protocol-oriented programming (POP) is a paradigm that employs 'protocols' or 'interfaces' to design software. It's a step away from traditional Object-Oriented Programming, allowing programmers to focus on behavior rather than type or classification.

2.1. Understanding the Basics

In the world of software development, there are two dominant paradigms: Object-Oriented Programming (OOP) and Functional Programming (FP). However, Protocol-Oriented Programming (POP) offers an exciting alternative that combines the strengths of both these approaches.

POP is built upon the concept of protocols. A protocol is a blueprint that defines methods, properties, or other requirements that suit a particular task or chunk of functionality. Protocols are a way to define interfaces in your code.

2.2. The Origin of Protocol-Oriented Programming

Protocol-oriented programming was introduced by Apple in 2015. They realized that while modern programming languages, such as Swift, are highly influenced by object-oriented paradigms, there are situations where an object-oriented approach might not be the most suitable. The reason for this is that OOP can at times introduce unnecessary complexity due to its reliance on inheritance hierarchies. To offer an alternative, Swift implements protocols, a crucial tool for enforcing conformity across different types. The use of protocols for structuring software forms the basis for protocol-oriented programming.

2.3. What Makes POP Unique?

Protocol-oriented programming offers the facility to add default behavior within protocols themselves by using protocol extensions. This feature allows developers to share default code across multiple classes or structures without necessarily using inheritance—leading to more modular, reusable and maintainable code. Moreover, protocols can be adopted by any type—class, enumeration, or structure alike—that can lead to a more flexible coding approach.

2.4. Key Components of Protocol-Oriented Programming

Chapter 3. Protocols

At its core, a protocol describes a blueprint of methods, properties, and other requirements for a particular piece of functionality. A protocol can then be adopted by a class, structure, or enumeration to provide implementations of the requirements.

```
protocol FullyNamed {
    var fullName: String { get }
}
```

In the example above, the `FullyNamed` protocol requires an instance property `fullName` of the type String.

Chapter 4. Protocol Adoption

Once a protocol is defined, it can be adopted by a structure or class.

```
struct Person: FullyNamed {
    var fullName: String
}


let me = Person(fullName: "John Doe")
```

In this example, the `Person` structure adopts the `FullyNamed` protocol.

Chapter 5. Protocol Extensions

Protocols can be extended to provide a base implementation of their behavior. This behavior can then be specialized by conforming types.

```swift
protocol RandomNumberGenerator {
    func random() -> Double
}

extension RandomNumberGenerator {
    func random() -> Double {
        return Double(arc4random()) / Double(UInt32.max)
    }
}
```

Chapter 6. Protocol Inheritance

Protocols can be designed to inherit one or multiple other protocols.

```swift
protocol Named {
    var name: String { get }
}

protocol Aged {
    var age: Int { get }
}

protocol NamedAndAged: Named, Aged {
}
```

6.1. Practical Applicability of Protocol-Oriented Programming

POP has some significant benefits in practical software development, including the provision of shared default behavior, avoidance of many problems related to traditional class-based inheritance hierarchies, and it fosters an easy-to-reuse and modular codebase.

Popularity for protocol-oriented programming sprouted mainly in Swift programming for iOS app development. However, its concepts hold potential usability in many other situations and languages. For instance, in languages like Python and Java, the concept of interfaces plays a similar role to protocols.

Protocol-oriented programming encourages the design of small, single-purpose entities that can be combined in various ways. This capability helps to create a codebase that is more flexible, easier to maintain, and reduces the complexity of the system. It can also make your code easier to test—smaller, focused protocols can be easily mocked during unit testing.

Moreover, when considering multi-threading and concurrent programming, the value types mainly used in protocol-oriented design reduce the risk of data races. This feature further increases the system's robustness.

Making the shift towards a protocol-oriented approach may seem daunting initially due to its abstract nature. However, with continuous practice and meticulous approach, the rewards of protocol-oriented programming will steadily become more evident.

In conclusion, mastering protocol-oriented programming can become a significant asset in a programmer's toolkit. As our software systems grow in complexity, having a more granular, flexible mechanism to enforce behavior across different types will undoubtedly prove beneficial. By the end of this journey, you should not only feel comfortable crafting custom protocols but also understand when and where to best apply protocol-oriented concepts.

Chapter 7. The Evolution of Object-Oriented to Protocol-Oriented

Our coding journey begins with an exploration of traditional object-oriented programming (OOP), understanding its principles, strengths, and weaknesses.

Object-oriented programming, or OOP, was a revolutionary paradigm that developers embraced in the early 1980s. This model represented a significant departure from previous procedural or functional programing, giving birth to a world of classes, objects, encapsulation, polymorphism, and inheritance.

7.1. Encapsulation and Data Hiding

Encapsulation, one of the cornerstones of OOP, shields an object's state and behavior, exposing only the necessary interfaces for interacting with the object's methods and properties. OOP languages, with their access modifiers (public, private, and protected), facilitate this level of data hiding and access control, reducing the likelihood of unwanted side effects from erroneous manipulation.

7.2. Inheritance

Another fundamental feature of OOP is inheritance, enabling classes to inherit properties and methods of existing ones, thereby promoting code reusability. Inheritance also empowers subclasses to override or extend the superclasses' methods and properties.

7.3. Polymorphism

Polymorphism is the ability of objects to take on many forms. By leveraging method overriding (runtime polymorphism) and overloading (compile-time polymorphism), developers are empowered to manipulate objects of different types through a unified interface.

Despite these advantages, OOP is not free of limitations. First, its inherent nature encourages tight coupling of data and behaviors, which can become a hurdle in maintaining and modifying code. Secondly, OOP can lead to monolithic and rigid class hierarchies, particularly when used incorrectly, resulting in fragile code, susceptible to breakage upon changes in ancestor classes.

These factors, among others, have led to a quest for an alternative paradigm, one that is more flexible, yet retains the benefits of OOP. Enter 'Protocol-Oriented Programming' (POP).

7.4. Introduction to Protocol-Oriented Programming

While object-oriented programming has dominated software development for years, protocol-oriented programming, introduced in Swift, has gained traction due to its uniqueness. POP borrows fundamental aspects from OOP, such as encapsulation, but it tackles inheritance and polymorphism differently, offering a more adaptable and powerful setting for structuring and organizing code.

7.5. Protocols and Structs

In POP, protocols provide a blueprint that, like interfaces in other languages, can define methods, properties, and other specifications, but their purpose goes well beyond defining contract for classes. In

Swift's protocol-oriented model, structs, classes, and even enums can conform to protocols, replacing the traditional class hierarchy with a more flexible and reusable model.

7.6. Protocol Extensions

POP takes protocol utility a step further with protocol extensions, enabling the default implementation of methods within protocols themselves. This feature provides something similar to multiple inheritance while avoiding diamond problems and other issues associated with the multiple inheritance in OOP.

7.7. Protocol Composition

Protocol composition is another powerful feature of POP. It offers the possibility to work with instances that conform to a combination of multiple protocols by producing more reusable and loosely coupled code.

In essence, by eschewing the strictness of inheritance, replacing classes with value types (struct, enums), and allowing for protocol extensions, protocol-oriented programming presents a compelling alternative to object-oriented programming. With a focus on composition over inheritance and a more loose coupling, POP increases the robustness, clarity, and maintainability of your code.

7.8. The Paradigm Shift

It's not a mere coincidence that Swift, an Apple's language, hails as a "protocol-oriented" language; it signifies a broader shift from a deep-rooted object-oriented programming approach. A journey from object-oriented to protocol-oriented programming involves a transition in approach: from consolidating functionality via broad and dense class hierarchies, to thinly spreading functionality across lean yet powerful protocols.

This journey doesn't discredit OOP's merits; rather, it amplifies those, dwells on the weaknesses, and puts forth a new paradigm that combines the best of both worlds - OOP and POP. The success of this transition isn't so much an absolute displacement, but the establishment of a coexistence mode where both OOP and POP find their optimal use cases.

They say evolution happens through gradual, minuscule changes over a long period. This transition from object-oriented to protocol-oriented programming embodies that, as a step by step process, progressing a bit more with each newly understood concept, hence why there is no direct leap to mastery. The understanding of object-oriented principles aids embracing the protocol-oriented programming model, even seeking it as an evolution, an improvement on the familiar constructs of OOP.

Such dexterity in moving from an object-oriented to a protocol-oriented paradigm is key to becoming a versatile software development professional, prepared for the ever-evolving, dynamic landscape of programming.

Chapter 8. Understanding Protocols: The Backbone of POP

Protocol, an integral cornerstone in Swift's Protocol-Oriented Programming (POP), is synonymous with conceptual blueprints for methods, properties, and other functionalities required by a specific task or piece of functionality. POP emboldens programmers to use protocols and protocol extensions, furthering a 'protocol first' discipline in software architecture. This chapter builds a robust understanding of protocols, genuinely appreciating their role in the fabric of POP.

8.1. What are Protocols?

Protocols, in Swift, define a blueprint which paves the definitive guide for methods, properties, and other functionalities pertinent to a specific functional requirement. These protocols can be adopted by classes, structures, and enumerations to stipulate the obligations that a conforming type must satisfy.

To declare a protocol, we use the `protocol` keyword. Below, we create a simple protocol named `Identifiable`.

```
protocol Identifiable {
    var id: String { get }
}
```

This protocol stipulates the requirement for a read-only property `id` of type `String`.

8.2. Conforming to Protocols

When a class, struct, or enumeration adopts a protocol, that type pledges to implement those requirements declared in the protocol. This is known as conforming to a protocol.

Let's create a User struct conforming to the Identifiable protocol:

```swift
struct User: Identifiable {
  var id: String
}
```

Our User struct fulfills the Identifiable protocol requirements, indicating that it bears an id property of type String.

8.3. Protocol Inheritance

Swift allows protocols to inherit one or more other protocols, effectively combining their requirements. A protocol can inherit from multiple protocols and can add further requirements on top of the requirements it inherits, creating a protocol hierarchy.

```swift
protocol Employee: Identifiable {
  var name: String { get }
  var department: String { get }
}
```

Here, Employee protocol inherits from Identifiable protocol and adds two more requirements: name and department.

8.4. Protocol Composition

In contrast to class-based programming languages that do not support multiple inheritance, Swift's protocol composition empowers the creation of complex types by combining multiple protocols.

```swift
protocol Named {
    var name: String { get }
}

protocol Aged {
    var age: Int { get }
}

struct Person: Named, Aged {
    var name: String
    var age: Int
}
```

8.5. Extending Protocols

Protocols can be extended to provide default implementations of requirements, add optional requirements, or add functionality beyond the protocol's declaration, effectively providing shared functionality for conforming types.

```swift
extension Identifiable {
    var idWithPrefix: String {
        return "ID: \(id)"
    }
}
```

Here we're adding a computed property to the `Identifiable` protocol.

Any conforming `Identifiable` type will now have `idWithPrefix` property.

8.6. Protocols as Type

A protocol can be used as a type to create highly flexible systems. When used as a type, the value it holds adheres to the protocol's requirements, providing abstraction and flexibility.

```swift
func displayID(of item: Identifiable) {
  print("ID is: \(item.id)")
}
```

By treating a protocol as a type, the function `displayID` can accept any conforming type to `Identifiable`.

8.7. Using Protocol Conformance in Practice

To illustrate the concept, consider a simple game system. Our game consists of different entities like `Player`, `Enemy`, `NonPlayerCharacter` (NPC). All entities conform to protocols `Living` and `Identifiable`.

```swift
protocol Living {
  var health: Int { get set }
}

struct Player: Living, Identifiable {
  var health: Int
  var id: String
}

struct Enemy: Living, Identifiable {
```

```
    var health: Int
    var id: String
}

struct NPC: Living, Identifiable {
    var health: Int
    var id: String
}
```

From this structure, we can create a function that operates on any
`Living` and `Identifiable` object.

```
func attack(target: inout Living) {
    target.health -= 10
}
```

This function accepts any conforming object to `Living` protocol and
decreases its health by 10, able to be called with any of the game
entities.

In this exploration of protocols, we unwrapped the pivotal role of
protocols in structuring the foundation for POP. This versatile tool in
Swift elevates software design by providing a level of flexibility and
abstraction, essential for the 'protocol-first' approach embodied in
POP.

Chapter 9. Creating Custom Protocols: First Steps

Creating custom protocols comprises an essential part of protocol-oriented programming. Each protocol declares a blueprint of methods, properties, and other requisites that suit a particular task or functionality. As the architect of these protocols, you are allowed to define the blueprints that other entities can adopt and conform to in your projects.

9.1. Understanding Protocols

A protocol in Swift, which is a popular language used for protocol-oriented programming, outlines a cohesive unit of methods, properties, and other requirements. These blueprints can be adopted by any type, be it class, enumeration or structure, to provide an actual implementation of the requirements. Protocols enable you to utilize type-agnostic way working, thereby allowing for more flexibility and extensibility in your programs as compared to traditional object-oriented approaches.

The protocol definition starts with the `protocol` keyword followed by the protocol's name:

```
protocol Vehicle {
}
```

This code snippet indicates an empty protocol named Vehicle. Even though it doesn't define any methods or properties yet, it can be used to create a type that suits special vehicular behavior.

9.2. Protocol Properties

The properties in a protocol are always declared as variables, and you are required to specify whether the property is gettable or gettable and settable. For instance:

```
protocol Vehicle {
    var speed: Int { get set }
    var isMoving: Bool { get }
}
```

In this piece of code, the protocol Vehicle has two properties: speed and isMoving. While the speed property can be set and retrieved, the isMoving property is read-only.

As you start creating your custom protocols, defining properties adds functionality and behavior to your protocol. Note that the protocol only asserts how the property appears, not how it should be stored or computed.

9.3. Protocol Methods

Similar to properties, protocols can require specific methods. A protocol method is declared similar to regular methods, but without curly braces or a method body. For instance:

```
protocol Vehicle {
    func startEngine()
    func moveAt(speed: Int)
}
```

In the above protocol, the two declared methods don't have an implementation. When a type declares this protocol, it needs to define these methods' bodies.

9.4. Protocol Adoption

Any type can adopt a protocol and provide an implementation for its requirements. After defining the protocol, the custom type's name can be followed by a colon and then the protocol name.

The process of conforming to protocols allows types to be more expressive and evolve more efficiently. It fosters code reuse and modular programming, which drastically increases the efficiency of developers.

```
class Car: Vehicle {
    var speed: Int
    var isMoving: Bool

    func startEngine() {
        // Implementation
    }

    func moveAt(speed: Int) {
        // Implementation
    }
}
```

In the example above, the Car class adopts the Vehicle protocol and defines all the requirements.

9.5. Protocols as Types

Create a parameter of a protocol type in a function that allows you to inject any conforming type. This function can then work with the protocol's methods and properties, and it doesn't care about the exact type that gets passed.

```
func race(vehicle: Vehicle) {
    // can call any method or access any property that
the Vehicle protocol declares
}
```

9.6. Inheritance in Protocols

One protocol can inherit from another. This action means a protocol can add to (or refine) the requirements of another protocol. You can even conform to multiple protocols at a time by listing them out, separated by commas.

In conclusion, protocol-oriented programming builds upon the principles of traditional object-oriented practice but elevates them by introducing flexibility, modularity, and expressivity. With this knowledge of creating custom protocols, you can start developing robust, dynamic, and efficient applications. Protocols stand at the foundation of implementing this paradigm, and mastering their creation is your first step towards cultivating resilient software architectures. We hope this guide has shed light on the process of creating custom protocols and has indeed driven you a step closer towards proficiency in protocol-oriented programming.

Chapter 10. Implementing Multiple Protocol Inheritance

Since you are asking for approximately five A4 pages of content, the response below is certainly not comprehensive. It gives you a conceptual overview of multiple protocol inheritance in protocol-oriented programming.

Protocol-oriented programming, leveraging Swift, empowers developers with unique features such as multiple protocol inheritance for structuring and fine-tuning systems. This guide outlines how to effectively design and implement it.

10.1. Understanding Multiple Protocol Inheritance

Just as classes inherit from superclasses in object-oriented programming, protocols can adopt other protocols. This gives rise to a concept known as multiple protocol inheritance. In essence, one protocol can inherit the requirements of multiple other protocols.

```
protocol ErrorReporting {
    func reportError()
}

protocol Logging {
    func logEvent()
}

protocol Debugging: ErrorReporting, Logging {
    func debug()
}
```

In this example, the Debugging protocol conforms to both the ErrorReporting and Logging protocols, implying that any entity adopting Debugging must fulfill requirements for ErrorReporting and Logging too.

10.2. Working with Multiple Protocol Inheritance

Working with multiple protocol inheritance requires correct structuring. Let's consider an example where we have a Car struct which adopts a Vehicle protocol. The Vehicle protocol inherits both the Engine and Tire protocols.

```
protocol Engine {
    func startEngine()
    func stopEngine()
}

protocol Tire {
    func inflateTire()
    func deflateTire()
}

protocol Vehicle: Engine, Tire {
    func startVehicle()
    func stopVehicle()
}

struct Car: Vehicle {
    func startEngine() {
        // Implement startEngine functionality here
    }

    func stopEngine() {
```

```swift
        // Implement stopEngine functionality here
    }

    func inflateTire() {
        // Implement inflateTire functionality here
    }

    func deflateTire() {
        // Implement deflateTire functionality here
    }

    func startVehicle() {
        startEngine()
        inflateTire()
        // Implement additional starting procedures
    }

    func stopVehicle() {
        stopEngine()
        deflateTire()
        // Implement additional stopping procedures
    }
}
```

In this scenario, Car adopts the Vehicle protocol which, in turn, conforms to the Engine and Tire protocols.

10.3. Practical Use Case of Multiple Protocol Inheritance

While this concept may seem straightforward, its applications are wide-ranging and practical. Using Swift, let's create a scenario in an e-commerce application where a Product needs to follow various protocols, such as Shipable, Taxable and Discountable.

```swift
protocol Shipable {
    var shippingCost: Double {get set}
    func shippingTime()
}

protocol Taxable {
    var taxAmount: Double {get set}
    func calculateTax()
}

protocol Discountable {
    var discount: Double {get set}
    func applyDiscount()
}

protocol Product: Shipable, Taxable, Discountable {
    var productName: String {get set}
    var productPrice: Double {get set}
}

struct Book: Product {
    var shippingCost: Double
    var taxAmount: Double
    var discount: Double
    var productName: String
    var productPrice: Double

    // Define all required methods of adopted protocols
    // ...
}
```

The struct `Book` confirms to the `Product` protocol, which inherits `Shipable`, `Taxable`, and `Discountable`. Therefore, `Book` adopts functionalities from all.

10.4. Key Considerations for Implementing Multiple Protocol Inheritance

There are key considerations that will improve your protocol-driven design:

1. **Code Organization:** The effectiveness of multiple protocol inheritance lies in well-organized, modular code. Each protocol should encapsulate a single aspect or behavior to keep the code readable and easily understood.

2. **Avoid Overlapping Functionality:** Make sure protocols being inherited do not overlap in functionality. Each protocol should have clearly distinct responsibilities to minimize redundancy.

3. **Protocol Composition:** If a type conforms to multiple protocols, use Swift's protocol composition feature instead of creating a new protocol that inherits from several others.

While multiple protocol inheritance can seem daunting initially, practice will build a deeper understanding and proficiency in this paradigm. By strategically structuring protocols and implementing across your software architectures, you will reap the rewards of reusable, cleaner and more robust code.

Chapter 11. POP in Practice: Real-World Use Cases

As we traverse further into our exploration of protocol-oriented programming (POP), we will now direct our attention towards practical, real-world use cases. After all, understanding the theoretical concepts can only take you so far; the true mastery lies in implementing them effectively in real projects.

11.1. Understanding Swift Protocols

Swift brought us protocol-oriented programming, extending traditional object-oriented programming methodology. Swift protocols are somewhat analogous to interfaces in languages like Java but with greater capability. They allow us to define a blueprint of methods, properties, and other requirements that suit a particular task or piece of functionality. With protocol-oriented programming, protocols can be adopted by classes, structs, and enums, giving us true behavioral and structural flexibility.

11.2. Protocols In Networking

When it comes to structuring code base for networking in Swift, protocols can save us from repeating code and make our architecture scale better. Consider a situation where we have a number of endpoints (URLs) that our app uses to communicate with a server.

```swift
protocol Endpoint {
    var baseURL: String { get }
    var path: String { get }
}
```

In the above example, we define an `Endpoint` protocol that declares two requirements: `baseURL` and `path`. Outlining protocols for our endpoints helps in segregating responsibilities and ensuring cleaner, more organized code.

11.3. Leveraging POP in UI

POP can also be extensively leveraged to delegate logic encapsulation within UI elements. Imagine a scenario where we want to set up a collection of `UIButton` with different corner radius and colors. Without POP, we would have to manually set up each button. With POP, we let a protocol do all the work for us:

```swift
protocol RoundButton {
    var cornerRadius: CGFloat { get set }
    var fgColor: UIColor { get set }
}

extension RoundButton where Self: UIButton {
    mutating func setup() {
        self.backgroundColor = fgColor
        self.layer.cornerRadius = cornerRadius
    }
}
```

In the example above, a protocol `RoundButton` is defined having properties `cornerRadius` and `fgColor`. An extension to this protocol is created where we add a function `setup()`. This function can now be used to easily set up any button conforming to `RoundButton`.

11.4. Protocols for Multi-Threading

Protocols can be used in Swift to make multi-threading code cleaner and leave fewer margins for error. They can be used to minimize the complexity and improve the readability of the routines that coordinate and manage threads.

Consider a scenario where we have multiple threads loading data from a network and writing it to a database. Each thread has to lock the database before writing to avoid dirty writes. Without protocols, every developer must remember to lock the database and release the lock after use. With protocols, we ensure that this always happens:

```swift
protocol ThreadSafety {
    var lock: NSLock { get set }
    func performThreadSafe(_ operation: () throws ->
Void) rethrows
}

extension ThreadSafety {
    func performThreadSafe(_ operation: () throws ->
Void) rethrows {
        lock.lock()
        defer { lock.unlock() }
        try operation()
    }
}
```

In the protocol `ThreadSafety`, a function `performThreadSafe(_ :)` is declared which performs operations in a thread-safe manner.

In conclusion, protocol-oriented programming is a powerful approach that Swift offers. It promotes code scalability, readability, and maintainability. When implemented strategically, it can help build robust, highly adaptable products, confining complexity and enhancing clarity.

Remember, every technology and technique has its ideal use case and it's our task as developers to find them and make the best possible use out of them.

Chapter 12. Mastering Protocol Extensions

In the world of protocol-oriented programming, protocol extensions are a real game-changer, bridging the gap between protocols and a traditional class-based inheritance model. They allow us to define default behavior for methods and provide a means to share code across multiple struct, enum, or class types that conform to a particular protocol.

12.1. Getting Started with Protocol Extensions

Protocol extensions are a way of defining default behavior for methods, in addition to providing an avenue for sharing code across multiple types. They act as a cornerstone for reusability and component software development.

In essence, a protocol extension is similar to a regular extension in Swift; however, it extends a protocol rather than a type. Any type that conforms to the protocol will automatically gain this default implementation without any additional code.

To define a protocol extension, we use the `extension` keyword followed by the protocol's name:

```swift
protocol SomeProtocol {
  // Protocol definition goes here
}


extension SomeProtocol {
    // Default method and property implementations
```

```
    }
```

Bear in mind that the default behavior can be overridden by the conforming type.

12.2. The Benefit of Using Protocol Extensions

In Swift, class inheritance is a fundamental building block, allowing behaviors and characteristics to be passed down from one class to another, but it has its limitations. Protocol-oriented programming with protocol extensions surmounts these by enabling a more flexible form of shared behavior.

Protocol extensions provide us with:

- The ability to define a blueprint of methods, properties, and other requirements.

- Default implementations to leverage shared behavior.

- Capability of extending protocols to provide sophisticated functionality in a flexible and modular manner.

These benefits empower developers to design safer, more efficient code that is easy to read, understand, and maintain.

12.3. When to Use Protocol Extensions

Protocol extensions can be particularly useful when you want to define a behavior that is common across many types, but perhaps not all instances of these types. For example, an 'Equatable' protocol might be applied to both 'Apple' and 'Orange' structs. You can then implement a default 'isEqual' function in a protocol extension, which can be overridden by the structs if needed.

Protocol extensions also shine when working with collection types because they can provide a high level of abstraction. For instance, you could define a protocol 'Summable' with an extension providing a default 'sum' function applied to any collection where the elements conform to 'Summable'.

12.4. How to Override Default Behavior

While protocol extensions offer a default behavior, there might be cases where a specific type needs a unique implementation. You can override the default behavior by providing its implementation in the conforming type.

Remember, the implementation in the conforming type always takes precedence over the default implementation in the extension.

12.5. Making the Most of Protocol Extensions

Protocol extensions can be powerful, but they also require thoughtful use. Here are a few best practices to guide their usage:

- Strive for small, focused protocols: This makes your code easier to reason about.

- Use protocol extensions when behavior varies: If all types handle a method in the same way, encoding that directly in a protocol extension can reduce code repetition.

- Be cautious with default implementations: Keep in mind that adding default implementations to a protocol extension effectively makes those methods optional, which may not always be the desired effect.

Embracing these practices will guide you towards making the most of protocol extensions, leading to cleaner and more organized code.

Protocol-oriented programming and protocol extensions are critical paths towards writing better, more adaptable, and reusable code. Equipped with this newfound knowledge and practical tips, you are ready to create more resilient software designs. Dive deeper, practice often, and enjoy the beauty of protocol extensions in your programming journey.

Chapter 13. Optimizing Software Design with Protocols

In the vast expanse of software development, protocols play a crucial role in emphasizing flexible design. This portion investigates and details the significance of protocols in software design and provides insights on how to optimize them, thereby ensuring robust, adaptable, and efficient systems.

13.1. Protocol Oriented Design

Protocol-oriented design is a paradigm that places protocols at the core of your software structure. This design tactic focuses on defining one or multiple protocols for each element or aspect needing implementation. These general protocols are then conformed to by specific classes, structs, or enums, providing customizable behavior devoid of the limitations associated with inheritance.

Therefore, when contemplating the structure of your software, shifting the design focus towards protocols not only results in a flexible structure but also encourages the creation of reusable and interoperable components. Protocol-oriented design is particularly beneficial for enabling polymorphism, metamorphosing complex classes, and surpassing the restrictions of type-based inheritance.

Let's consider a simple example:

```
protocol Flyable {
    var speed: Double { get }
}
```

```
struct Bird: Flyable {
    let speed: Double
}

struct Plane: Flyable {
    let speed: Double
}
```

In this example, `Flyable` is a protocol with a property `speed`. The structures `Bird` and `Plane` both conform to the `Flyable` protocol and hence, adopt the `speed` property. This way, both `Bird` and `Plane` could be utilized wherever a `Flyable` protocol is required, showcasing polymorphism.

13.2. Extension Driven Development

In a protocol-oriented design approach, extensions play a paramount role. Swift's extension feature enables you to add new functionalities, provide default implementations, or extend existing types' capacities. A single protocol can have multiple extensions, either within the same scope or spread across different files, endorsing flexibility.

Implementing extension-driven development brings in a sea of advantages, from code reusability and maintainability, clutter reduction to facilitating test-driven development. Below is a simulation of using an extension to provide a default implementation of a protocol:

```
protocol Flyable {
    var speed: Double { get }
    func fly() -> String
}

extension Flyable {
```

```
    func fly() -> String {
        return "Flying at a speed of \(speed)"
    }
}
```

In this example, the `fly` function is provided a default
implementation in the `Flyable` protocol's extension. Existing or new
types conforming to this protocol automatically inherit this
implementation. The default implementation could be overridden if
needed.

13.3. Adopting Protocol Compositions

13.3.1. Multiprotocol Approach

Protocols assist in creating granular, shared behavior across multiple
types. They enable you to form a relationship between types that
might not share a common ancestry, capacitating you to create
protocols specific to certain behaviors or properties and then
composing them as needed. Swift allows the design and
implementation of types conforming to multiple protocols, known as
multiprotocol conformance, thereby providing more flexible and
granular design:

```
protocol Flyable {
    var speed: Double { get }
}


protocol Breathable {
    var oxygenRequired: Double { get }
}
```

```
struct Bird: Flyable, Breathable {
    let speed: Double = 25.0
    let oxygenRequired: Double = 1.5
}
```

There are two protocols - Flyable and Breathable. The structure Bird simultaneously conforms to both protocols. This scenario exhibits software design on a behavior basis, and not merely on the structures or classes.

13.3.2. Protocol Composition Type

When declaring a variable that needs to conform to multiple protocols, the & sign suggests the composition of two or more protocols:

```
protocol Flyable {}
protocol Breathable {}


let bird: Flyable & Breathable
```

Such design practices amplify behavioral design, streamline codes, and yield flexible software structures with reusable components.

13.4. Protocol and Associated Types

An additional layer of abstraction can be added to protocols in Swift using associated types. They provide a placeholder name for a type to be used as part of the protocol. The actual type to be used is not specified until the protocol is adopted. This allows for greater flexibility and declares relationships between methods and properties in your protocols.

Pictorial representation of associated type usage is as follows:

```
protocol Storable {
    associatedtype ItemType
    mutating func append(_ item: ItemType)
    subscript(i: Int) -> ItemType { get }
}
```

These strategies elevate protocols to a higher level of abstraction, thereby allowing for more refined and adaptable software design.

In conclusion, protocol-oriented programming is a powerful tool that imparts flexibility to the design and implementation of software architectures. By focusing on the conformance to protocols rather than inheritance, combined with the advantage of extensions, protocol compositions and associated types, software designs can be both optimally built and effortlessly readjusted. This approach facilitates making changes as minimal as possible by isolating variation, resulting in code that is less prone to bugs and easier to understand and maintain. protocol-oriented programming helps create code that is prepared for future adaptations and alterations, making this paradigm a smart choice for software design.

Chapter 14. Effective Strategies for Debugging Protocols

Before diving headfirst into techniques for debugging protocols, it is necessary to understand that debugging is an integral aspect of the software development process. It's a vital skill that aids developers in identifying, tracking, and rectifying errors, consequently enabling the development of robust and seamless applications. This process becomes slightly more nuanced when dealing with protocols due to their abstract nature. However, fear not for we are here to unravel the complexities of debugging protocols.

14.1. Understanding Protocol Behaviors

To begin debugging, it's crucial to understand the behavior of protocols. A protocol defines a set of methods and properties that a particular concrete type (be it a class, a struct, or an enum) adheres to. It can also declare properties to be either gettable, settable, or both. It's important to remember that protocols only describe what methods and properties a conforming type should have, but they don't implement these functionalities by themselves.

Consider a 'Drivable' protocol:

```
protocol Drivable {
    var speed: Double { get set }
    func startEngine()
    func stopEngine()
}
```

Any object that conforms to this 'Drivable' protocol must have a 'speed' property, a 'startEngine()' method, and a 'stopEngine()' method.

Understanding the behavior of the protocol aids in identifying any breaking changes during the debugging process.

14.2. Debugging with Protocol Extensions

Protocol extensions can provide default implementations of the methods and properties declared in the protocol. In other words, if a conforming type doesn't provide its own implementation of a protocol method, the default implementation from the extension is used.

Let's extend the 'Drivable' protocol:

```
extension Drivable {
    func startEngine() {
        print("The engine has started.")
    }
}
```

Now, all objects that conform to 'Drivable' will have a 'startEngine()' method—unless the object itself provides its own implementation of 'startEngine()'.

It is important to be very careful while proving default implementations in protocol extensions as not specifically providing custom implementations for your types can sometimes lead to the execution of undesired default functionality when the protocol methods are invoked.

14.3. Inspecting Protocol Compliance

The dynamic nature of Swift allows for conformance to be checked and cast at runtime using the `is` and `as` operators. For example:

```swift
let myCar: Drivable = Car()
// Check if myCar conforms to Drivable
if myCar is Drivable {
    print("This car is drivable.")
    myCar.startEngine()
}
```

This is especially useful in debugging because it allows checking which concrete type adheres to a protocol. This way, you can ensure that a specific object adheres to a protocol, which can prevent potential crashes due to non-compliance. To pinpoint missing protocol conformance, exceptions can be placed in the code where a non-complying object is attempting to access a protocol's functionality.

14.4. Debugging Inherited Protocols

Swift also allows a protocol to inherit one or more existing protocols, which can also challenge the debugging process:

```swift
protocol Electric {
    func rechargeBattery()
}

protocol ElectricDrivable: Drivable, Electric {
    // Inherits from Drivable and Electric
```

```
}
```

In cases like this, debugging protocol conformance can be tricky. Adding breakpoints to the methods defined in the protocol will help you ensure that they are called as expected.

14.5. Debugging Optional Protocol Methods

In Swift, all methods declared in a protocol are required for compliance. However, one can use the @optional directive when defining protocols, transforming these directives from being required to optional.

In the protocol below, the method changeTires() is optional:

```
@objc protocol Drivable {
    var speed: Double { get set }
    func startEngine()
    @objc optional func changeTires()
}
```

When debugging protocols with optional methods, using breakpoints can help identify whether an object calls the optional method when expected to, or skips calling it altogether. Deep introspection of these optional methods can also be achieved using Swift's reflection API.

Mastering the art of debugging protocols necessitates understanding, practice, and patience. However, once accomplished, it can greatly enhance the development process, paving the way for well-crafted, resilient software systems. The debugging techniques shared in this chapter, when well harnessed, can help you gracefully side-step pitfalls associated with protocol compliance, inherited protocol implementations, and even the subtleties of utilizing optional methods in protocols. Happy debugging!

Chapter 15. Futuristic Perspectives: The Impact of POP on Emerging Languages

In the cutting-edge landscape of technology, the protocol-oriented programming (POP) paradigm is shaping the evolution and future of emerging languages. This influence is perceptible in the refining of existing languages and the genesis of new ones, just as the profound impact of object-oriented programming (OOP) mechanisms has altered language evolution.

15.1. How POP Influences Language Constructs

Languages that support POP have a notable distinction in their foundational constructs. Unlike OOP, where inheritance and classes are the base elements, POP languages emphasize definitions of protocols. A protocol declares methods and properties that encapsulate particular tasks and functionality. Unlike the 'is-a' relationship in class-based OOP, in POP, it's about 'can do' relationships which adds to the flexibility.

Notably, features such as default implementations and associated types, inherent in POP languages, add a layer of abstraction without high inheritance costs. This feature allows programmers to create more flexible, reusable and stable code bases.

15.2. Case Study: Swift

To understand the impact of POP on emerging languages, let's focus on Swift, Apple's successor to Objective-C. This language incorporates the principles of POP and offers several advantages.

Swift's adoption of POP is a clear departure from the class-dependency problem of Objective-C. This move defined Swift's identity as a language that makes extensive use of protocols rather than inheritance, promoting composition over inheritance.

Extensions are another significant feature in Swift's POP approach. Extensions allow the addition of new functionality to existing class, struct, enumeration or protocol types, which makes for a highly flexible coding methodology.

15.3. Future Prospects Influenced by POP

Interestingly, emerging languages that incorporate POP principles continue the tradition of blending paradigms. It's becoming increasingly common to see multiparadigm languages that marry procedural, functional, and POP methodologies to enhance flexibility and productivity.

For instance, Julia, Rust, and Go, while not fully embracing POP, exhibit a preference for interfaces and traits, demonstrating the influence of POP thinking. Hence, this solidifies the argument that POP will continue to shape the aspect of emerging languages.

15.4. Adaptability to the Internet of Things (IoT)

In the Internet of Things (IoT) realm, where a multitude of devices with limited resources are interconnected, POP plays a pivotal role. The composition methodology of POP enhances the highly distributed and dynamic nature of IoT by reducing the complexity of involved relationships. This is so because interfaces and functions are easier to manage and debug in comparison to inheritance hierarchies.

15.5. Synergy with Microservices Architecture

The rise in popularity of Microservices Architecture also places POP in a pivotal position. With separate services communicating over simple mechanisms, the use of interfaces is preferred over inheritance structures. POP's 'contract-based' approach aligns well with the loosely coupled nature of Microservices networks.

15.6. Conclusion

As we analyse the prospective vista of programming paradigms, it's evident that POP has carved and will continue to etch an impactful place in the lexicon of emerging languages. With its emphasis on flexibility, adaptability, and stability, POP is finding resonance in multiple programming and technological realms, promising a bright future in the world of software development. The impact of POP is not merely ideological. It's practical, logical, and key to developing software that's resilient, robust, and scalable. As we delve further into the future, it's expected that more languages will incorporate POP constructs, refining the way we approach programming.

www.ingramcontent.com/pod-product-compliance
Lightning Source LLC
Chambersburg PA
CBHW071003260726

48661CB00007B/2763